A 30-Day Journey Through
the True Woman Manifesto

And who knows whether you
have not come to the kingdom
for such a time as this?

—Esther 4:14

CONTENTS

4 How to Use This Booklet

6 What Is the True Woman Manifesto All About?

10 The True Woman Manifesto

15 30-Day Devotional

50 The True Woman Movement

How to Use This Booklet

The True Woman Manifesto is meant to be lived out in your everyday life. But how do you make a manifesto personal and practical? *A 30-Day Journey Through the True Woman Manifesto* is designed to help you do just that.

You Can Expect This on Every Page:

ICON KEY

transcript

audio

article

blog

book

video

product

- A focused statement from the True Woman Manifesto
- Scripture references to study that day's statement
- One or two "making it personal" questions to help you apply the statement to your life
- Space to journal your response to the question(s)
- Recommended content to help you further explore each statement

Suggestions When Journeying Alone:

- Pray. Ask God to speak to you from His Word.
- Read (or better yet, study) the Scriptures that relate to each point. Don't rush—linger in God's Word.
- Journal your thoughts and responses to the questions.
- Visit TrueWomanManifesto.com to listen to the teachings; read the transcripts, articles, and blogs; or watch the videos related to that day's statement.
- Pray some more. Ask the Lord to continue showing you His heart and ways, how you can best love and enjoy Him, and specific ways you can glorify Him today.

Suggestions When Journeying with Others:

- Pray about who should join you on this journey. Ask God for teachable women who are eager to grow in Christ.
- Consider how you can make this a "Titus 2 moment" by inviting both younger and older women to journey with you. Invite one or many; any size can work.
- Be purposeful and realistic. Meet at a convenient time and a place conducive to meaningful conversation.
- Come ready. Encourage everyone to read the Scripture and manifesto statement(s) and to do some journaling ahead of time.
- Stay on topic and stay on target.
- Encourage everyone to be a good listener, to keep things confidential, to avoid gossiping and grumbling, and to be considerate and careful when offering advice.
- Let God's Word be your true source of authority when difficult questions arise.
- Pray, pray, and then pray some more. Pray that God's Spirit will work in all your hearts.

For the best experience, download the digital version of this booklet at
TrueWomanManifesto.com

What Is the True Woman Manifesto All About?

Let's just say it right from the start: you can't live the True Woman Manifesto. You'll quickly find it's too hard, too difficult. As you read through it, you'll likely be thinking, *I could never live up to all that!* You know what? You can't. None of us can.

Living up to the Manifesto—or God's Word—isn't something you can do. You cannot be God's true woman on your own. As Nancy Leigh DeMoss says,

> *"We don't have the capacity, the desire, the ability to be this kind of woman. We are utterly dependent on the grace of God and the power of His Spirit living within us to be the kind of woman we are talking about."*

The True Woman Manifesto is about the grace of the Lord Jesus Christ—His gospel—invading your life and giving you the grace to take the beauty and wonder of Christ and this Good News to your world . . . as a woman.

Since 2008, tens of thousands of women have signed the Manifesto. They've said, "Yes, Lord! We want to be women who reflect the heart of Christ in this way."

> "I have read [the True Woman Manifesto] more than once and regard it as a faithful, clear, true, wise, indeed magnificent document. What an amazing thing it would be if hundreds of thousands of women signed on with their hearts."
>
> —John Piper—

The True Woman Manifesto is comprised of thirty-five statements—each based on Scripture—and is designed to be fleshed out in your daily life. This little booklet in your hands will help you and others personalize the Manifesto. We trust you'll be encouraged as you take your time going through the Manifesto—but you'll also likely find it a challenge, and yes, convicting too.

The True Woman Manifesto was developed to be a concise statement of core aspects of what it means to be a true woman of God. With principles drawn from the Word of God, it's a lens, a way of looking at some of the foundational aspects of what it means to live as a Christian woman.

The True Woman Manifesto has three "movements":

- First, it lays a foundation which is true for everyone's life, whether male or female.
- Secondly, it speaks to the authority of Scripture as the source that reveals God's pattern for womanhood.
- Finally, it digs into God's design for your life as a woman and how you can best fulfill His desires.

So, the True Woman Manifesto is a practical message that really does affect every area of your life. It speaks to:

- the way you think
- your worldview and perspective
- the way you respond to pressure
- your values and priorities

- your commitments
- the way you talk to women and men
- the way you show respect to others created in the image of God

As Nancy Leigh DeMoss says, "Every area of our lives is impacted by whether or not we live out God's design for our lives as women." This is what the True Woman Manifesto is all about.

In your heart and in your home—and in the hearts and homes of Christian women all around this world—a movement of revival and reformation is needed "for such a time as this" (Esther 4:14).

"The True Woman Manifesto is not meant to be a comprehensive statement of faith, nor an infallible guide to every aspect of life, nor a document that in any way adds to or replaces Scripture. The True Woman Manifesto is merely a signpost highlighting some major points about what we believe the Bible says to women and declaring our conviction that even if its teachings are unpopular in this day and age, the Bible provides the best (and wholly authoritative) instruction with regards to what we believe and how we live as women."

—Mary Kassian—

TRUE WOMAN
manifesto

A personal and corporate declaration of belief, consecration, and prayerful intent—to the end that Christ may be exalted and the glory and redeeming love of God may be displayed throughout the whole earth

WE BELIEVE that God is the sovereign Lord of the universe and the Creator of life, and that all created things exist for His pleasure and to bring Him glory.

WE BELIEVE that the creation of humanity as male and female was a purposeful and magnificent part of God's wise plan, and that men and women were designed to reflect the image of God in complementary and distinct ways.

WE BELIEVE that sin has separated every human being from God and made us incapable of reflecting His image as we were created to do. Our only hope for restoration and salvation is found in repenting of our sin and trusting in Christ who lived a sinless life, died in our place, and was raised from the dead.

WE REALIZE that we live in a culture that does not recognize God's right to rule, does not accept Scripture as the pattern for life, and is experiencing the consequences of abandoning God's design for men and women.

WE BELIEVE that Christ is redeeming this sinful world and making all things new, and that His followers are called to share in His redemptive purposes as they seek, by God's empowerment, to transform every aspect of human life that has been marred and ruined by sin.

As Christian women, we desire to honor God by living counter-cultural lives that reflect the beauty of Christ and His gospel to our world.

TO THAT END, WE AFFIRM THAT. . .

SCRIPTURE is God's authoritative means of instructing us in His ways and it reveals His holy pattern for our womanhood, our character, our priorities, and our various roles, responsibilities, and relationships.

WE GLORIFY GOD and experience His blessing when we accept and joyfully embrace His created design, function, and order for our lives.

AS REDEEMED SINNERS, we cannot live out the beauty of biblical womanhood apart from the sanctifying work of the gospel and the power of the indwelling Holy Spirit.

MEN AND WOMEN are both created in the image of God and are equal in value and dignity, but they have distinct roles and functions in the home and in the church.

WE ARE CALLED as women to affirm and encourage men as they seek to express godly masculinity, and to honor and support God-ordained male leadership in the home and in the church.

MARRIAGE, as created by God, is a sacred, binding, lifelong covenant between one man and one woman.

WHEN WE RESPOND humbly to male leadership in our homes and churches, we demonstrate a noble submission to authority that reflects Christ's submission to God His Father.

SELFISH INSISTENCE on personal rights is contrary to the spirit of Christ who humbled Himself, took on the form of a servant, and laid down His life for us.

HUMAN LIFE is precious to God and is to be valued and protected, from the point of conception until rightful death.

CHILDREN are a blessing from God, and women are uniquely designed to be bearers and nurturers of life, whether it be their own biological or adopted children, or other children in their sphere of influence.

GOD'S PLAN for gender is wider than marriage; all women, whether married or single, are to model femininity in their various relationships, by exhibiting a distinctive modesty, responsiveness, and gentleness of spirit.

SUFFERING is an inevitable reality in a fallen world; at times we will be called to suffer for doing what is good—looking to heavenly reward rather than earthly comfort—for the sake of the gospel and the advancement of Christ's Kingdom.

MATURE CHRISTIAN WOMEN have a responsibility to leave a legacy of faith, by discipling younger women in the Word and ways of God and modeling for the next generation lives of fruitful femininity.

BELIEVING THE ABOVE, we declare our desire and intent to be "true women" of God. We consecrate ourselves to fulfill His calling and purposes for our lives. By His grace and in humble dependence on His power, we will:

1. Seek to love the Lord our God with all our heart, soul, mind, and strength.

2. Gladly yield control of our lives to Christ as Lord—we will say "Yes, Lord" to the Word and the will of God.

3. Be women of the Word, seeking to grow in our knowledge of Scripture and to live in accord with sound doctrine in every area of our lives.

4. Nurture our fellowship and communion with God through prayer—in praise, thanksgiving, confession, intercession, and supplication.

5. Embrace and express our unique design and calling as women with humility, gratitude, faith, and joy.

6. Seek to glorify God by cultivating such virtues as purity, modesty, submission, meekness, and love.

7. Show proper respect to both men and women, created in the image of God, esteeming others as better than ourselves, seeking to build them up, and putting off bitterness, anger, and evil speaking.

8. Be faithfully engaged in our local church, submitting ourselves to our spiritual leaders, growing in the context of the community of faith, and using the gifts He has given us to serve others, to build up the Body of Christ, and to fulfill His redemptive purposes in the world.

9. Seek to establish homes that manifest the love, grace, beauty, and order of God, that provide a climate conducive to nurturing life, and that extend Christian hospitality to those outside the walls of our homes.

10. Honor the sacredness, purity, and permanence of the marriage covenant whether ours or others'.

11. Receive children as a blessing from the Lord, seeking to train them to love and follow Christ and to consecrate their lives for the sake of His gospel and Kingdom.

12. Live out the mandate of Titus 2—as older women, modeling godliness and training younger women to be pleasing to God in every respect; as younger women, receiving instruction with meekness and humility and aspiring to become mature women of God who in turn will train the next generation.

13. Seek opportunities to share the gospel of Christ with unbelievers.

14. Reflect God's heart for those who are poor, infirm, oppressed, widows, orphans, and prisoners, by reaching out to minister to their practical and spiritual needs in the name of Christ.

15. Pray for a movement of revival and reformation among God's people that will result in the advancement of the Kingdom and gospel of Christ among all nations.

A personal and corporate declaration of *belief, consecration, and prayerful intent—to the end that Christ may be exalted and the glory and redeeming love of God may be displayed throughout the whole earth.*

DAY 1

I BELIEVE that *God is the sovereign Lord* of the universe and the Creator of life, and that all created things exist for His pleasure and to bring Him glory.

MAKE IT PERSONAL

Is the glory of God your supreme passion? Does it define your goals, objectives, how you spend your time . . . everything about you? If not, what does?

DIG INTO SCRIPTURE

- 1 Cor. 8:6
- Col. 1:16
- Rev. 4:11

Journal

_____
_____
_____
_____
_____
_____
_____
_____
_____
_____
_____
_____
_____
_____
_____
_____

GO DEEPER

"The Reason You Exist" *by Nancy Leigh DeMoss*

"El-Shaddai: The All-Sufficient One" *by Nancy Leigh DeMoss*

"Who Are You God?" *by Erin Davis*

DAY 2

I BELIEVE that the creation of humanity as *male and female was a purposeful and magnificent* part of God's wise plan, and that men and women were designed to reflect the image of God in complementary and distinct ways.

MAKE IT PERSONAL

How does the truth that men and women are created in the image of God speak to the chronic feelings of inferiority and worthlessness that many women experience?

DIG INTO SCRIPTURE

- Gen. 1:26–27; 2:18
- 1 Cor. 11:8

Journal

_____

_____

_____

_____

_____

_____

_____

_____

_____

_____

_____

_____

_____

GO DEEPER

"Recovering from a Gender Earthquake" by Nancy Leigh DeMoss

"The Danvers Statement on Biblical Manhood and Womanhood" by The Council on Biblical Manhood and Womanhood

"Gender Matters" Panel

"Complementarianism for Dummies" by Mary Kassian

DAY 3

I BELIEVE that *sin has separated every human being from God* and made us incapable of reflecting His image as we were created to do. Our only hope for restoration and salvation is found in repenting of our sin and trusting in Christ who lived a sinless life, died in our place, and was raised from the dead. *I REALIZE* that we live in a culture that does not recognize *God's right to rule*, does not accept Scripture as the pattern for life, and is experiencing the consequences of abandoning God's design for men and women.

MAKE IT PERSONAL

Have I trusted in the grace of God and the shed blood of Christ to save me, apart from any good works I may have done? How is this impacting my daily life? Are there any specific ways you need to lean into the authority of God's Word, embrace God's priorities and purposes for your life and home, and live out the beauty and the wonder of womanhood as God created it to be?

Journal

DIG INTO SCRIPTURE

- Gen. 3:1–7, 15–16
- Prov. 14:12
- Jer. 17:9
- Mark 1:15
- Rom. 3:18; 8:6–7
- 1 Cor. 15:1–4
- 2 Tim. 3:16

GO DEEPER

"Are You Wearing Fig Leaves?" *by Nancy Leigh DeMoss*

"We Have Been Approved" *by Carrie Gaul*

"A Vision for Biblical Womanhood" *by Nancy Leigh DeMoss*

"12 Questions to Help You Discern Truth from Error" *by Nancy Leigh DeMoss*

DAY 4

I BELIEVE that ***Christ is redeeming this sinful world*** and making all things new, and that His followers are called to share in His redemptive purposes as they seek, by God's empowerment, to transform every aspect of human life that has been marred and ruined by sin.

MAKE IT PERSONAL

Today do I realize that I am under "new ownership," that I have been "bought with a price," and that I belong to God? How might God use my life to make a difference in this world?

DIG INTO SCRIPTURE

- Eph. 4:22–24
- Col. 3:12–14
- Titus 2:14

Journal

_____

_____

_____

_____

_____

_____

_____

_____

_____

_____

_____

_____

_____

GO DEEPER

 "You Are Invited Back to a Garden" *by Nancy Leigh DeMoss*

"Snake in My Garden" Panel

"A Call to Biblical Womanhood" by Nancy Leigh DeMoss

"How to Change" by Nancy Leigh DeMoss

DAY 5

SCRIPTURE is *God's authoritative means of instructing us* in His ways, and it reveals His holy pattern for our womanhood, our character, our priorities, and our various roles, responsibilities, and relationships.

MAKE IT PERSONAL

Do I spend time daily sitting at the feet of Jesus, listening to His Word, and worshiping Him? Do I earnestly seek to learn more of the heart, will, and ways of God on a regular basis?

DIG INTO SCRIPTURE
- Josh. 1:8
- 2 Tim. 3:16
- 2 Pet. 1:20–21
- 3:15–16

Journal

GO DEEPER

☑ 🎧 "God Makes Himself Known" *by Nancy Leigh DeMoss*

☑ 🎧 "The Wonder of the Word" *by Nancy Leigh DeMoss*

☑ 🎧 "Getting into the Word and Getting the Word into You" *by Nancy Leigh DeMoss*

💬 "One Mom's Journey (with Four Little Ones) Through the Bible" *by Carrie Ward*

DAY 6

I GLORIFY GOD and experience His blessing when I *accept and joyfully embrace His created design*, function, and order for my life.

MAKE IT PERSONAL

Have you wholeheartedly said yes to God's design for you as a woman? Is there any part of your heart that feels reluctant or is holding back?

DIG INTO SCRIPTURE

- 1 Tim. 2:9
- Titus 2:3–5
- 1 Pet. 3:3–6

Journal

GO DEEPER

☑ ∩ "Turning the Spotlight Toward God" *by Nancy Leigh DeMoss*

☑ ∩ "God's Beautiful Design for Women: Titus 2:1–5, Part 1" *by Nancy Leigh DeMoss*

📺 "The Ultimate Meaning of True Womanhood" *by Dr. John Piper*

📺 "Sugar and Spice" Panel

WE BELIEVE that God is the sovereign Lord of the universe and the Creator of life, and that all created things exist for His pleasure and to bring Him glory.

DAY 7

AS A REDEEMED SINNER, I cannot live out the beauty of biblical womanhood apart from the sanctifying work of the gospel and the power of the indwelling Holy Spirit.

MAKE IT PERSONAL

Am I seeking a fresh, daily filling of the Holy Spirit in my life? How do I need to depend on the power of the Holy Spirit this week to be and to do that for which God has chosen me?

DIG INTO SCRIPTURE

- John 15:1–5
- 1 Cor. 15:10
- Eph. 2:8–10
- Phil. 2:12–13

Journal

GO DEEPER

📝 🎧 "You Can't Be a True Woman (On Your Own)" *by Nancy Leigh DeMoss*

📝 🎧 "Divine Anointing" *by Nancy Leigh DeMoss*

📖 "Mary: Portrait of a Woman Used by God" *by Nancy Leigh DeMoss*

💬 "The Best Friend a Girl Could Want" *by Erin Davis*

DAY 8

MEN AND WOMEN are both created in the image of God and are *equal in value and dignity*, but they have distinct roles and functions in the home and in the church. *I AM CALLED* as a woman to affirm and encourage men as they seek to express godly masculinity and to honor and *support God-ordained male leadership* in the home and in the church.

MAKE IT PERSONAL

Who are the men God has placed in your life (home, workplace, church, etc.)? What are some specific ways you can help them glorify God? What are some ways you're building these men up or tearing them down?

DIG INTO SCRIPTURE

- Gen. 1:26–28, 2:18
- Mark 9:35; 10:42–45
- 1 Cor. 14:34
- Gal. 3:26–28
- Eph. 5:22–33
- 1 Tim. 2:12–3:7
- 1 Pet. 5:1–4

Journal

GO DEEPER

- "Does the Bible Belittle Women?" *by Nancy Leigh DeMoss*
- "Relationships Teach Submission to God" *by Nancy Leigh DeMoss*
- "Men and Women in the Church" *by Nancy Leigh DeMoss*
- "The Dance of Complementarity" *by Mary Kassian*

DAY 9

MARRIAGE, as created by God, is a sacred, binding, *lifelong covenant* between one man and one woman.

MAKE IT PERSONAL

If you're married, how are you investing in and nurturing the heart of your marriage? Do you frequently express admiration and gratitude to your husband?

DIG INTO SCRIPTURE

- Gen. 2:24
- Mark 10:7–9

Journal

GO DEEPER

- "A God-Sized Picture of Marriage" *by Nancy Leigh DeMoss*
- "What Does Your Marriage Communicate?" *by Nancy Leigh DeMoss*
- "Marriage Through Gospel Eyes" *by Jani Ortlund*
- "Hope for the Hopeless Marriage" *by Kimberly Wagner*

DAY 10

WHEN I RESPOND humbly to male leadership in my home and church, I demonstrate a *noble submission to authority* that reflects Christ's submission to God His Father.

MAKE IT PERSONAL

What are some ways I need to wait for God to work in and through the authorities He has placed in my life?

DIG INTO SCRIPTURE

- Eph. 5:22–33
- 1 Cor. 11:3

Journal

_____

_____

_____

_____

_____

_____

_____

_____

_____

_____

_____

_____

_____

_____

GO DEEPER

- "What Submission Does and Does Not Mean" *by Nancy Leigh DeMoss*

- "Confident, Strong, and Submissive" *by Nancy Leigh DeMoss*

- "Liberated Through Submission" *by Bunny Wilson with Nancy Leigh DeMoss*

- "Whoa—Not the 'S' Word" *by Kimberly Wagner*

DAY 11

SELFISH INSISTENCE on personal rights is contrary to the spirit of Christ who **humbled Himself,** took on the form of a servant, and laid down His life for me.

MAKE IT PERSONAL

Have you been acting more like a temporary servant of God or like His willing and permanent slave? How so? Would you go to Him in prayer and commit your whole life, present and future, to Him?

DIG INTO SCRIPTURE

- Luke 13:30
- John 15:13
- Eph. 4:32
- Phil. 2:5–8

Journal

GO DEEPER

☑ ∩ "Will You Lay Down Your Rights?" *by Nancy Leigh DeMoss*

☑ ∩ "Servant of the Lord" *by Nancy Leigh DeMoss*

📖 "41 Evidences of Pride" *by Nancy Leigh DeMoss*

📖 "How's Your Love Life" *by Nancy Leigh DeMoss*

WE BELIEVE that the creation of humanity as male and female was a purposeful and magnificent part of God's wise plan, and that men and women were designed to reflect the image of God in complementary and distinct ways.

DAY 12

HUMAN LIFE is precious to God and is to be *valued and protected* from the point of conception until rightful death. **CHILDREN** are a blessing from God; women are uniquely designed to be *bearers and nurturers of life*, whether it be their own biological or adopted children or other children in their sphere of influence.

MAKE IT PERSONAL

Are you or your children being entertained by movies, shows, or video games that sensationalize or trivialize murder or that promote a cheapened view of life? If so, could it be possible that you're not as pro-life as you think? Can you identify any ways you have bought into culture's faulty perspectives on children?

DIG INTO SCRIPTURE

- Gen. 1:28; 9:1
- Psalm 127, 139:13–16
- Titus 2:4–5

Journal

_____

_____

_____

_____

_____

_____

_____

_____

_____

GO DEEPER

- "Why Is Human Life Precious?" *by Nancy Leigh DeMoss*
- "Are Children Truly a Blessing from the Lord?" *by Nancy Leigh DeMoss*
- "Epicenter: The World-Changing Impact of a Christ-Centered Home" *by Bill & Holly Elliff*
- "Motherhood Or Singleness: Which Is More Sanctifying?" *by Colleen Chao*

DAY 13

GOD'S PLAN for gender is wider than marriage; all women, whether married or single, are to *model femininity* in their various relationships by exhibiting a distinctive modesty, responsiveness, and gentleness of spirit.

MAKE IT PERSONAL

What negative reaction or fears might the thought of being feminine evoke in you? What benefits and blessings could result from embracing femininity?

DIG INTO SCRIPTURE

- 1 Cor. 11:2–16
- 1 Tim. 2:9–13

Journal

GO DEEPER

✒ 🎧 "The Core of Femininity" *by Nancy Leigh DeMoss*

✒ 🎧 "The Beauty of Meekness" *by Nancy Leigh DeMoss*

✒ 🎧 "The Beauty of a Modest Heart" *by Nancy Leigh DeMoss*

📖 "Your Philosophy Is Showing" *by Nancy Leigh DeMoss*

DAY 14

SUFFERING is an inevitable reality in a fallen world; at times we will be ***called to suffer*** for doing what is good—looking to heavenly reward rather than earthly comfort—for the sake of the gospel and the advancement of Christ's Kingdom.

MAKE IT PERSONAL

How might God call me to suffer in order that Jesus' redeeming life might be experienced by others? Am I willing?

DIG INTO SCRIPTURE

- Matt. 5:10–12
- 2 Cor. 4:17
- James 1:12
- 1 Pet. 2:21–23; 3:14–17; 4:14

Journal

GO DEEPER

- "Perspective on Suffering" by Nancy Leigh DeMoss
- "Finding God in the Desert" by Nancy Leigh DeMoss
- "How to Endure Suffering" by Nancy Leigh DeMoss
- "Lessons from 'The Devastation'" by Erin Davis

DAY 15

MATURE CHRISTIAN WOMEN have a responsibility to leave a legacy of faith by *discipling younger women* in the Word and ways of God and modeling for the next generation lives of fruitful femininity.

MAKE IT PERSONAL

Do I feel a personal sense of responsibility for the spiritual condition of the next generation? Who am I praying persistently and fervently for? How am I making a conscious effort to ensure that they walk with God?

DIG INTO SCRIPTURE

- Titus 2:3–5

Journal

_____

_____

_____

_____

_____

_____

_____

_____

_____

_____

_____

_____

GO DEEPER

- ☑ ∩ "God Calls All Different Types of Mothers" by Nancy Leigh DeMoss

- ☐ "What Is a True Woman?" by Nancy Leigh DeMoss

- ☑ ∩ "Spiritual Mothering" by Susan Hunt

- ☑ ∩ "Teaching Biblical Womanhood to Teens" by Mary Kassian & Susan Hunt

| DAY 16 | Seek to *love the Lord* my God with all my heart, soul, mind, and strength. |

MAKE IT PERSONAL

Do you long for greater intimacy with Christ? How can you experience and nurture a closer relationship with Him?

DIG INTO SCRIPTURE

- Deut. 6:4–5
- Mark 12:29–30

Journal

GO DEEPER

- "The Most Important Commandment" by Nancy Leigh DeMoss
- "How to Fall and Stay in Love with Jesus" by Nancy Leigh DeMoss
- "Craving God's Best" by Erin Davis
- "The Quiet Place" by Nancy Leigh DeMoss

WE BELIEVE that sin has separated every human being from God and made us incapable of reflecting His image as we were created to do. Our only hope for restoration and salvation is found in repenting of our sin and trusting in Christ who lived a sinless life, died in our place, and was raised from the dead.

| DAY 17 | Gladly *yield control* of my life to Christ as Lord—I will say "Yes, Lord" to the Word and the will of God. |

MAKE IT PERSONAL

Was there ever a time I made myself fully available to God, for whatever purposes He might want to use my life? If so, am I still living like that?

DIG INTO SCRIPTURE

- Psalm 25:4–5
- Rom. 6:11–13, 16–18;
- Eph. 5:15–17

Journal

_____

_____

_____

_____

_____

_____

_____

_____

_____

_____

_____

_____

GO DEEPER

- "The Battle for Control" by Nancy Leigh DeMoss
- "Surrender: The Heart God Controls" by Nancy Leigh DeMoss
- "Lessons Learned in the Flea House" by Kimberly Wagner
- "Take My Life and Let It Be" by Nancy Leigh DeMoss

DAY 18

Be a *woman of the Word*, seeking to grow in my knowledge of Scripture and to live in accord with sound doctrine in every area of my life.

MAKE IT PERSONAL

Do I love the Word of God? Do I use the Word in the midst of real-life situations? If not, do I need to commit to spending more time reading it, memorizing it, meditating on it, and sharing it with others?

DIG INTO SCRIPTURE

- Acts 17:11
- 1 Pet. 1:15
- 2 Pet. 3:17–18
- Titus 2:1, 3–5, 7

Journal

_____

_____

_____

_____

_____

_____

_____

_____

_____

_____

_____

_____

_____

_____

_____

GO DEEPER

 "Women of the Word" by Nancy Leigh DeMoss

"Learn to Discern: How to Recognize and Respond to Error in the Culture" by Nancy Leigh DeMoss

"Who Are You Lord, And What Do I Do? " by Jennifer Cortez

"A Place of Quiet Rest" by Nancy Leigh DeMoss

DAY 19

Nurture my fellowship and *communion with God* through prayer—in praise, thanksgiving, confession, intercession, and supplication.

MAKE IT PERSONAL

Am I a woman of prayer? Do I respond to the circumstances and challenges of each day by expressing gratitude for the greatness and mercy of God?

DIG INTO SCRIPTURE

- Psalm 5:2
- Phil. 4:6
- 1 Tim. 2:1–2

Journal

GO DEEPER

"Walking and Talking with God" by Nancy Leigh DeMoss

"How Do You Pray Without Ceasing?" by Nancy Leigh DeMoss

"The Lord's Prayer" by Nancy Leigh DeMoss

Take a Prayer Challenge by *Revive Our Hearts*

DAY 20

Embrace and express my *unique design and calling* as a woman with humility, gratitude, faith, and joy.

MAKE IT PERSONAL

Am I conscious that anything good or useful about my life is the result of God's undeserved grace poured out on me? What am I believing God for that is impossible apart from His power?

DIG INTO SCRIPTURE

- Prov. 31:10–31
- Col. 3:18
- Eph. 5:22–24, 33b

Journal

_____

_____

_____

_____

_____

_____

_____

_____

_____

_____

_____

_____

_____

_____

_____

_____

GO DEEPER

 "Every Cell in Your Body" by Nancy Leigh DeMoss

"The Attitude of Gratitude" by Nancy Leigh DeMoss

"The 30-Day Choosing Gratitude Challenge" by Revive Our Hearts

"Reversing the Downhill Trend of Gratitude" by Nancy Leigh DeMoss

DAY 21

Seek to glorify God by *cultivating such virtues* as purity, modesty, submission, meekness, and love.

MAKE IT PERSONAL

Am I pure in my behavior—my relationships; what I watch, read, and listen to; the way I dress? How do I need to grow in purity in my motives, thoughts, and private habits?

DIG INTO SCRIPTURE

- Rom. 12:9–21
- 1 Pet. 3:1–6
- 1 Tim. 2:9–14

Journal

_____

_____

_____

_____

_____

_____

_____

_____

_____

_____

_____

_____

_____

_____

_____

_____

_____

GO DEEPER

"Develop Virtue by Being Rather Than Doing" by Nancy Leigh DeMoss

"Characteristics of a Meek and Quiet Spirit" adapted from Matthew Henry

"Biblical Portrait of Womanhood" by Nancy Leigh DeMoss

"Excuse Me? How We've Gotten the Motivation for Purity All Wrong" by Paula Hendricks

WE REALIZE that we live in a culture that does not recognize God's right to rule, does not accept Scripture as the pattern for life, and is experiencing the consequences of abandoning God's design for men and women.

DAY 22

Show proper *respect* to both men and women, created in the image of God, by esteeming others as better than myself; seeking to build them up; and putting off bitterness, anger, and evil speaking.

MAKE IT PERSONAL

What would your family, friends, and colleagues say about your words? Do they generally encourage or discourage? Who can you intentionally encourage today?

DIG INTO SCRIPTURE

- Eph. 4:29–32
- Phil. 2:1–4
- James 3:7–10; 4:11

Journal

_____

_____

_____

_____

_____

_____

_____

_____

_____

_____

_____

_____

GO DEEPER

- "The Way to Make Men Feel Respected" by Nancy Leigh DeMoss

- "The Power of Words" by Nancy Leigh DeMoss

- "Do You Need Some Conversation Peace? Ask Yourself These Twenty Questions" by Mary Kass

- Take the 30-Day Husband Encouragement Challenge by Revive Our Hearts

DAY 23 Be faithfully *engaged in my local church*, submitting myself to my spiritual leaders, growing in the context of the community of faith, and using the gifts He has given me to serve others, to build up the Body of Christ, and to fulfill His redemptive purposes in the world.

MAKE IT PERSONAL

Who am I accountable to spiritually? Do I make it easy for them to lead me? How could I express appreciation and gratitude to my spiritual leaders today for their labors on my behalf?

DIG INTO SCRIPTURE

- Rom. 12:6–8; 14:19
- Eph. 4:15, 29
- Heb. 13:17

Journal

_____
_____
_____
_____
_____
_____
_____
_____
_____
_____
_____
_____

GO DEEPER

- "A Body, a Building, a Family, and a Bride" by Nancy Leigh DeMoss

- "Follow the Leaders" by Nancy Leigh DeMoss

- "Opportunities for Women" by Dr. John Piper

- "How to Get the Most Out of Your Pastor's Preaching" by Nancy Leigh DeMoss

DAY 24

Seek to establish a home that manifests the love, grace, beauty, and order of God; that provides a climate conducive to nurturing life; and that *extends Christian hospitality* to those outside the walls of my home.

MAKE IT PERSONAL

Does God's design for you to be the welcoming keeper of your home call for any adjustments in your heart or habits? If so, what might that look like?

DIG INTO SCRIPTURE

- Prov. 31:10–31
- 1 Tim. 5:10
- 1 John 3:17–18

Journal

GO DEEPER

- "A Climate Conducive to Life" by Nancy Leigh DeMoss
- "The Heart of Hospitality" by Nancy Leigh DeMoss
- "Hospitality and the Gospel: Earning Trust, One Meal at a Time" by Liz Lockwood
- "Inhospitable Hospitality" by Erin Davis

DAY 25 Honor the sacredness, purity, and permanence of the *marriage covenant*—whether mine or others'.

MAKE IT PERSONAL

Is it possible that you might be endangering your purity and the purity of the men you know? Spend time this week talking and praying with other godly women about how you can help protect your purity and others.

DIG INTO SCRIPTURE

- Matt. 5:27–28
- Mark 10:5–9
- 1 Cor. 6:15–20
- Heb. 13:4

Journal

GO DEEPER

- "A Commitment to Permanence" by Nancy Leigh DeMoss
- "Personal Hedges" by Nancy Leigh DeMoss
- "Sexual Purity" by Nancy Leigh DeMoss
- "Girls Gone Wise in a World Gone Wild" by Mary Kassian with Nancy Leigh DeMoss

DAY 26 Receive children as a ***blessing from the Lord,*** seeking to train them to love and follow Christ and to consecrate their lives for the sake of His gospel and Kingdom.

MAKE IT PERSONAL

What can you do today to cultivate a heart even more like Jesus' heart toward children (Matt. 18:10)?

DIG INTO SCRIPTURE

- Psalm 127:3
- Prov. 4:1–23; 22:6

Journal

GO DEEPER

- "Why Are Children a Blessing?" by Nancy Leigh DeMoss
- "Raising Kids for the Glory of God" by Ann Dunagan
- "Does God Have a Plan for Your Family?" by Holly Elliff
- Take the 30-Day Mom Makeover Challenge by Erin Davis

WE BELIEVE that Christ is redeeming this sinful world and making all things new, and that His followers are called to share in His redemptive purposes as they seek, by God's empowerment, to transform every aspect of human life that has been marred and ruined by sin.

DAY 27 Live out the mandate of Titus 2—as an older woman, *modeling godliness* and training younger women to be pleasing to God in every respect; as a younger woman, receiving instruction with meekness and humility and aspiring to become a mature woman of God who in turn will train the next generation.

MAKE IT PERSONAL

Which "older" woman's example, counsel, or input are you currently benefitting from? Who are you diligently passing on God's truth to from the next generation? How could you be even more intentional about leaving a godly legacy?

DIG INTO SCRIPTURE

• Titus 2:3–5

Journal

GO DEEPER

☑ ∩   "Modeling and Training" by Nancy Leigh DeMoss

☑ ∩   "The Value of Older Women Teaching Younger Women" by Nancy Leigh DeMoss

☑ ∩   "Authentic Mentoring" by Donna Otto with Nancy Leigh DeMoss

💬   "Cracking the Code of Discipleship" by Jani Ortlund

DAY 28 — Seek opportunities to *share the gospel* of Christ with unbelievers.

MAKE IT PERSONAL

Do unsaved people in my neighborhood, my community, and my workplace know that I'm a Christian? How can my life and my lips share what a privilege it is to be a child of God?

DIG INTO SCRIPTURE
- Matt. 28:19–20
- Col. 4:3–6

Journal

_____
_____
_____
_____
_____
_____
_____
_____
_____
_____
_____
_____
_____
_____

GO DEEPER

- "Share What Jesus Is Doing in Your Life" by Nancy Leigh DeMoss
- "Rahab and the Thread of Redemption" by Nancy Leigh DeMoss
- "How I—An Atheist—Fell in Love with Jesus" by Heidi Jo Fulk
- "Defending the Faith" by Kimberly Wagner

DAY 29 Reflect God's heart for those who are poor, infirm, oppressed, widows, orphans, and prisoners by *reaching out* to minister to their practical and spiritual needs in the name of Christ.

MAKE IT PERSONAL

In general, am I more generous or stingy in sharing with others who are in need? Who can I bless this week with compassion, sacrifice, and acts of service?

DIG INTO SCRIPTURE

- Matt. 25:36
- Luke 10:25–37
- James 1:27
- 1 Tim. 6:17–19

Journal

GO DEEPER

- "Channels of God's Generosity" by Nancy Leigh DeMoss
- "Daughters of Hope" by Michelle Rickett with Nancy Leigh DeMoss
- "Hope for an Aching Heart, with Margaret Nyman" by Nancy Leigh DeMoss
- "Is a House in the Hood on Your Bucket List?" by Paula Hendricks

DAY 30

Pray for a movement of *revival and reformation* among God's people that will result in the advancement of the Kingdom and gospel of Christ among all nations.

MAKE IT PERSONAL

As you prayerfully consider God's conditions for revival in 2 Chronicles 7:14, ask yourself, "Is my life in such a state that God could be pleased to send revival to my heart, my home, my church, and my community?" If not, identify the area you need to grow in so that you can be a candidate for revival.

DIG INTO SCRIPTURE

- 2 Chron. 7:14
- Psalm 51:1–10; 85:6
- 2 Pet. 3:9

Journal

_____

_____

_____

_____

_____

_____

_____

_____

_____

_____

_____

GO DEEPER

- "When the Church Comes" by Nancy Leigh DeMoss
- "The Role of Prayer in Spiritual Awakening" by Nancy Leigh DeMoss
- "Preparing for Revival" by Nancy Leigh DeMoss
- "When Do We Need Revival?" by Nancy Leigh DeMoss

The True Woman Movement

We are believing God for a widespread personal and corporate revival and reformation among women. We long for a grassroots movement of Christ-centered revival and biblical womanhood, where women:

- Discover and embrace God's design and mission for their lives,
- Reflect the beauty and heart of Christ to their world,
- Intentionally pass on the baton of Truth to the next generation, and
- Pray earnestly for an outpouring of God's Spirit in their families, churches, nation, and world.

Revive Our Hearts and the True Woman Movement is all about calling women to freedom, fullness, and fruitfulness in Christ. Thanks for journeying with us!

Women's Ministry Leaders . . . We Are Here for You!

Whether you're a small group Bible study leader, pastor's wife, mentor, counselor, or women's ministry leader, it's our prayer that we can serve you as you serve others.

Often women's ministry leaders are under-trained, under-resourced, over-committed, and overlooked. It's our desire to help train, equip, encourage, connect, and mentor you in the role God has called you to fill.